THIS IS WHAT LOVE BECOMES

Love, Legacy, and the Beautiful Life We Built Together

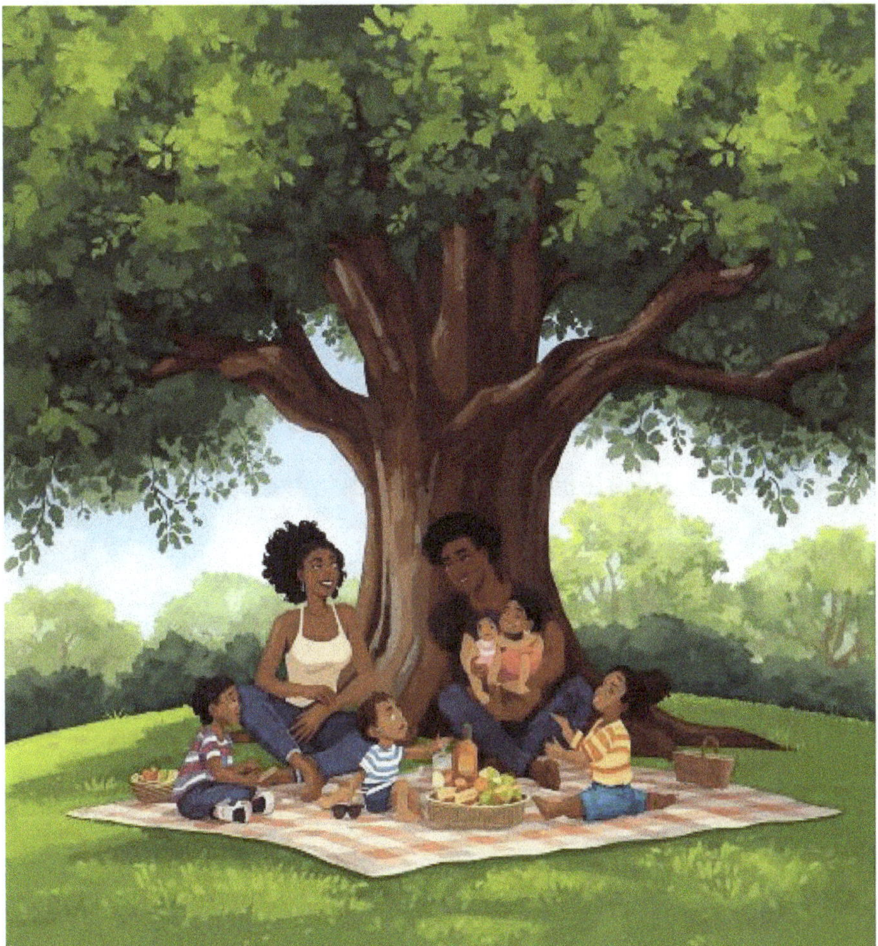

VGDAWSON

Books on Friendship, Relationships, and Personal Growth

Books on Personal Growth and Life Reflection

Unlocking Your Best Self

Setting Boundaries with Family & Friends

Books on Relationships and Personal Boundaries

My Best Friend

The Friendship Years

Books for Readers Life After 50

Ageless Connections

Who Will Cry For You?

Discover More

Visit the author online for additional books, resources, and inspiration:

www.what2buynext.com

This is What Love Becomes
Love, Legacy, and the Beautiful Life We Built Together
Copyright © 2026 by VaNessa G. Dawson

Published by
Second Season Press
Birmingham, Alabama
www.what2buynext.com
ISBN: 978-1-972518-17-5

Cataloging information is available from the Library of Congress.
Library of Congress Control Number: 2026912483
First Edition: 2026

Printed in the United States of America

Disclaimer

This book is intended for inspirational, motivational, and personal development purposes only. The stories, experiences, and reflections shared are not meant to replace professional counseling, therapy, legal guidance, or financial advice.

The author has taken great care to present insightful observations about love, partnership, legacy, and emotional growth. However, each reader's situation is unique, and individual circumstances may vary.

Readers are encouraged to seek professional guidance for any concerns related to mental health, relationship challenges, or life decisions requiring specialized support.

The author and publisher disclaim any liability for any loss, risk, or consequences incurred, directly or indirectly, from the use and application of the information contained in this book.

For every couple who chose each other
even when life tried to pull you apart.

For the men who made sacrifices quietly
and for the women who carried dreams boldly.

For the families built from patience, forgiveness,
shared effort, and unwavering love.

And for the generations who stand as living proof
of what two people can create
when the yoke is even
and the love is real.

This book is for you.
Your legacy matters.

Table of Contents

Some stories arrive softly, without warning.
Not in a dramatic speech, not in a planned moment, but in a peaceful place where life pauses just long enough for you to truly listen.

That is how this book began.

It started on a warm summer afternoon at a family reunion, four generations gathered in one park, laughter drifting across the air, children racing in the grass, elders sharing stories, and people from all walks of life coming together under one sky. In the middle of that joy, my friend and I sat at a picnic table, resting beneath the shade of a maple tree.

And that is where he told me his story.

Not the polished version.
Not the "tell it at weddings" version.
But the honest version, the one shaped by sacrifices, choices, compromise, tears, forgiveness, growth, and a love that lasted because it evolved.

He talked about dreams he let go of.

Dreams he resurrected later.

Partnership he had to learn.

Legacy he didn't realize he was building.

And the deep peace he eventually found.

What struck me most was not the details of his story, but the wisdom hidden inside it. Wisdom about what real love becomes when two people commit to building a life; not a perfect life, but a meaningful one.

Too often, we chase love that sparks but can't sustain.

We crave excitement but ignore stability.

We want passion but forget that peace is its own kind of beauty.

We romanticize the beginning of love, but rarely honor what it takes to make love last.

This book is a tribute to lasting love; the kind that grows quietly, matures gracefully, and stands tall over time. It is a celebration of partnership, legacy, and the small everyday choices that build a lifetime.

Through these chapters, I hope you find wisdom, reflection, healing, and truth.

I hope you recognize parts of your own journey; the dreams you've held, the dreams you've set aside, the sacrifices you've made, and the love you've honored.

Most of all, I hope this book reminds you that love is not just what you feel.

Love is what you build.
And this is what love becomes.

Chapter 1

The Picnic That Started the Conversation

There are certain summer days that don't ask for anything except your presence. No rushing, no deadlines, no problems tugging at your sleeve, just a gentle invitation to slow down and breathe in the moment.

That was the kind of day I was having when my friend invited me to his family reunion picnic. I didn't know what to expect. I thought it would be a small gathering of cousins and a few aunties, maybe a table with potato salad and somebody's famous peach cobbler.

I was wrong.

They didn't just invite family; they invited generations.

When we pulled up, it felt like we had driven into a living documentary. Four generations strong. Kids racing through the grass, elders sitting in shaded folding chairs telling stories with the kind of laughter that shakes the soul, teens pretending not to hear their names being called, grown folks catching up like they hadn't seen each other in twenty years, and music flowing from a speaker that had clearly lived through all four generations and survived every one of their reunions.

They had rented the entire park, and every corner was alive. One side smelled like ribs slow cooking on a charcoal grill. Another side smelled like a fish fry, the kind where the men argue about who seasons better but somehow all the fish tastes the same just like home.

Someone was frying chicken in a giant cast-iron pot, and over on the far side of the park, a group was steaming shrimp with Old Bay like it was a competition. There were tents, coolers, domino tables, card games, kids splashing near the water, and folks waving at us like we were cousins they hadn't met yet.

I stood there taking it all in.

The atmosphere was calming, inviting, pleasant, and peaceful. It had the kind of peace you don't have to earn; the kind that just settles on you the moment you arrive. Happiness does that sometimes. It sneaks up on you quietly.

As we walked through the park, my friend introduced me to everyone. And when I say everyone, I mean everyone.

People I had never seen a day in my life hugged me like I'd been missing from the reunion for the last three cycles.

Someone tried to hand me a plate before I could even say hello. That's how you know you're at a real family gathering, they feed you before they learn your name.

We walked for a while, making our way around the park, admiring the mix of cultures, accents, food traditions, and the easy way people blended together like they had known each other all their lives. I was soaking up the peace when we spotted an empty picnic table under a maple tree. The breeze was soft, the shade was perfect, and both of us were ready to sit down. Sometimes life speaks the loudest when you finally sit still.

The moment we settled, he let out a long sigh; not the tired kind, but the reflective kind. The kind of sigh you release when something in your heart has been waiting to speak.

He looked out at the families, the laughter, and the kids running in circles, and then said something that I didn't expect.

"You know," he began, "I never liked BBQ."

I blinked, thinking surely he was joking. We were literally sitting in the middle of the biggest BBQ, fish fry, chicken-cooking festival I'd ever seen. Smoke was in the air, ribs were falling off bones, and someone was yelling at a cousin for putting too much sauce on the chicken.

He wasn't joking.

"I never liked BBQ," he repeated. "And I never wanted to open a restaurant."

I just looked at him. This man had built a name for himself in the food business. People raved about his restaurant. He had a line out the door on Saturday nights. Folks ordered his ribs for holidays, weddings, and any event where pride was on the menu.

So I asked the only reasonable question:

"Then how in the world did you end up with a BBQ restaurant?"

He smiled, the slow, knowing smile of a man who has lived enough life to be honest without shame.

"I fell in love," he said.

And just like that, the conversation shifted from picnic chatter to something deeper.

He told me that the woman he fell in love with had a dream, owning her own restaurant. It wasn't his dream. He wanted a job where he could travel, take pictures, and see the world. But he loved her, truly loved her, and he wanted to be the kind of man who made her feel supported, encouraged, and believed in. He wanted to help her shine.

"So if I wanted to be with her," he said, "I had to become the type of man she needed, someone who could help make her dream real. Seeing her happy made me whole."

There was no bitterness in his voice. No regret. Just peace.

He talked about how they started small church festivals, food trucks, cookouts for local events. How she brought the recipes and the vision, and he brought the business sense, the planning, and the ability to get things done.
"She was the dream," he said, "and I became the structure."
Then he said something that stuck with me:

"We built this life together. Look at the family we made. Look at the friends who became family. Look at the life we share. This " he motioned around the park, "this is what love becomes when you build it right."

I felt that.

He wasn't talking about expensive gifts or grand gestures. He was talking about the slow, deliberate building of a life, days, years, decisions, sacrifices, forgiveness, and shared commitment. The kind of love that grows deeper, not louder.

As he continued, he said, "And you know the best part? I eventually got my dream too. Now we travel. Now we take pictures. Now we enjoy life without worrying about the budget. We both won."

That is the definition of an even yoke.

Two people pulling life together at the same pace, with the same strength, toward the same purpose.
As he spoke, I looked around at those four generations, living proof of what one couple's choices can become.

Love, when nurtured, becomes legacy.

Legacy becomes culture.

Culture becomes family.

And family becomes the story people tell long after you're gone.

That day, sitting under that maple tree, eating food I didn't ask for and listening to stories I didn't expect, I realized something powerful:

Love isn't just what you feel.
It's what you build.

And sometimes the most beautiful versions of love are born quietly, at a picnic table, on a peaceful summer day, surrounded by generations who didn't even know they were part of the story.

Chapter 2

"I Never Even Liked BBQ": Dreams We Let Go

There's something disarming about honesty, not the polite kind, but the kind that catches you completely off guard. When my friend said, "I never liked BBQ," I felt my eyebrows lift so high they might've left my forehead.

How does a man who doesn't like BBQ become the unofficial king of ribs?

I couldn't help it — I laughed.
Not at him, but at the irony of it all.

He laughed too, that deep belly laugh of a man who has been telling that joke for years but still finds it funny.

"Everybody assumes I love it," he said. "I let them believe it."

Then he leaned back and sighed, the kind of sigh that comes only when truth is about to get real.

"You ever look at your life and say, 'How did I get here?' Not in a bad way... just in a 'this wasn't the plan' kind of way?"

I nodded. Oh, I understood.

Sometimes life chooses for you before you know how to choose for yourself.

He told me that young adulthood is full of two things: unrealistic dreams and unrealistic confidence. His dream wasn't BBQ sauces and smoke pits. It wasn't early mornings chopping vegetables or figuring out who burned the chicken. His dream was simple.

"I wanted to see the world," he said. "I wanted to take pictures of everything. I wanted to wake up with a suitcase packed and not know where I'd end up next."

That was his heart speaking. You could hear the boy in him, the one who dreamed without limits. The one who didn't yet understand that dreams often get rearranged by love.

"But then," he said, "I met her."

Not in a movie-style way. No fireworks, no slow-motion moment with dramatic music. Just a normal day that became a turning point.

"She was talking about her dreams, and I knew right then… either I could walk beside her or watch someone else do it."

And just like that, the man who dreamed of cameras and travel learned how to marinate ribs.

That's how love works sometimes, quietly, humbly, with a soft shift that turns into a whole new life.

He wasn't forced.
He wasn't manipulated.
He wasn't guilted.

He chose it.

"I wanted her to feel supported. I wanted her to know someone who believed in her the way she believed in me."

He paused, then added with a smirk, "But let me be clear, that first year nearly took me out."

I laughed, because you could hear the truth in his voice.
Real partnership is not just sacrifice; it's adjustment.

He shared how he struggled with the long hours, the unpredictable income, the trial-and-error of figuring out a business neither one of them had ever run before. There were nights they both cried. Days they both wanted to quit. Weeks where quitting looked more attractive than staying.

"And I swear," he said, "I burned more meat that first year than I cooked right."

But here's the thing:
He stayed.
He learned.
And he found joy in the one place he never expected it; not in the BBQ itself, but in the way her face lit up when customers loved her food.

Sometimes the dream isn't the work.
Sometimes the dream is who you're building the work with.

He said something that stuck with me:

"You can let go of a dream when it's not your calling anymore."

That's the part we forget.

We treat childhood dreams like they're contracts written in stone, but life has a way of revealing which dreams were meant for growth and which ones were meant for identity.

He realized that traveling and photography were pieces of a younger version of himself. Beautiful pieces, yes. Meaningful pieces, yes. But they were not the whole story.

"I didn't lose myself," he said quietly. "I found a new version of me."

He became a businessman.
A leader.
A partner.
A husband.
A father.
A provider.
A man who learned that he didn't need to travel the world to find purpose; he built purpose right where he stood.

But don't get it twisted; he still held onto that dream deep down. And he didn't bury it out of resentment or obligation. He tucked it away like a seed that needed the right season to grow.

"That's why I don't regret a single decision," he said. "Some dreams take the long route."

He leaned forward and said, almost whispering,
"And when that season finally came... it felt better than it would've been in my twenties."

It hit me then:
Letting go doesn't always mean losing.
Sometimes it means making room for something better.

I asked him if he ever felt like he sacrificed too much. He shook his head before I even finished the question.

"Compromise is losing something. Sacrifice is giving something. I wasn't losing. I was giving."

There is a big difference.

We always talk about women sacrificing for love.
But men do it too; quietly, consistently, and without needing applause.

"You know what the funny part is?" he added, laughing again.

"People call me 'the BBQ man' like it's my identity. I don't even correct them."

I asked why.

"Because legacy isn't about what you love," he said. "It's about what you build."

That line stayed with me long after the picnic ended.

His life didn't follow his original script.
But he wrote a better story anyway.

A story where love wasn't a limitation; it was an expansion.
A story where his dream didn't die; it matured.
A story where partnership wasn't a burden; it was a blessing.

Dreams evolve.
People evolve.
And love, when done right, evolves with you.

The man who never liked BBQ built a life that fed an entire community; not just with food, but with trust, stability, and devotion.

And in the process, he discovered something more valuable than his original dream:

The joy of building something meaningful with someone who cherishes you.

This was only the beginning of what he shared with me that day.
And little did I know, the best part of his story was still waiting for us in the next conversation.

Chapter 3

Falling in Love With Someone's Dreams

People always talk about falling in love with someone's eyes, someone's laugh, someone's personality; but they rarely talk about falling in love with someone's dreams. Yet that's the quiet truth that holds most long-lasting relationships together. The heart may fall first, but the dreams… the dreams are what keep you staying.

My friend told me that when he met his wife, it wasn't her beauty that convinced him she was "the one" though he made sure to add, with a proud grin, that she was indeed beautiful. What captured him was the way she talked about her future. Not in a distant, wishful way. Not in a "one day, maybe" kind of way. But in a this is going to happen, and here's how kind of way.

"She had a fire," he said, leaning back at the picnic table. "And I had never seen anyone talk about a dream like that; like it already belonged to them."

That's the thing about vision:
You can hear it long before you see it.

He said she talked about opening a restaurant with the same passion a preacher has on Sunday morning. She had the menu planned, the dishes she wanted to serve, the sauce she wanted to perfect, even the colors she wanted on the walls. He said he was standing there thinking about taking pictures of mountains in another country, and here she was describing her life in full color like she was reading from a blueprint.

"It scared me a little," he admitted. "Not because her dream was big, but because mine suddenly felt small."

That's honesty most people won't admit.
When you meet someone who knows exactly where they're going, you start questioning whether you've been wandering around with your eyes closed.

But his next words made me smile.

"I didn't fall in love with her restaurant idea," he said. "I fell in love with the way she believed in herself."

There it was; the shift, the turning point.
Love didn't start in the kitchen.

It started in the confidence of a woman who knew her life had purpose.

He explained that people underestimate what it means to fall in love with someone who has a dream. It means entering their world, their way of thinking, their rhythm, their fears, their hopes. It means learning their language, their hunger, their reason for waking up early and going to bed late.

It means sacrificing the worst parts of yourself so the best parts of both of you can rise.

And yes; sometimes it means learning how to run a business you never asked for.

He laughed telling me about their early days dating; how every conversation somehow circled back to her restaurant. They'd be out at dinner, and she'd critique the menu layout. Drive past a building? She'd see potential. Visit another restaurant? That was "market research." He said he didn't even know he was studying for a test he never signed up for.

"But you know what?" he said, smiling softly. "Her passion rubbed off on me.

When someone believes in something that deeply, you start believing too; not because the dream is yours, but because they are.”

And there it is; what love becomes before the vows, before the bills, before the shared responsibilities:

Love becomes alignment.

Not that everything matches perfectly.
Not that dreams merge overnight.
Not that life suddenly gets easy.

But alignment, real alignment, happens when two people make a choice:

Your dream matters to me because you matter to me.

He told me he wanted her to shine. He wanted her to walk into her purpose without holding herself back. He wanted her to feel supported, not because he was trying to impress her, but because he saw who she could become. And it was beautiful to him.

"When you care about someone's dream," he said, "you're really caring about their future self."

I paused at that because it's true. Some people fall in love with who you are right now. But the rare ones; the ones who love deeply, they fall in love with who you're becoming.

And those are the relationships that last.

He said he knew she would become something incredible, and he wanted a front-row seat to witness it. So he adjusted. Not changed, adjusted. There is a big difference.

He didn't lose himself.
He stretched himself.

He didn't shrink.
He grew.

He didn't surrender his identity.
He expanded it to include hers.

That's what healthy love does; it stretches you into someone wiser, stronger, more patient, more capable than you were before.

Then he said something that hit me harder than I expected:

"I didn't fall in love with cooking. I fell in love with her joy. I fell in love with the way she lit up when she talked about her dream. I fell in love with the fact that she needed someone who would stand with her and I wanted to be that man."

That's partnership.
That's maturity.
That's unselfish love.

A relationship rooted in personal gain won't survive the storms of life.
A relationship rooted in shared purpose becomes unbreakable.

He said the day he realized he wanted to play a role in her dream was the day he knew he couldn't lose her. Because losing her meant losing the part of himself that had started to dream differently.

"It wasn't that I chose her dream over mine," he said. "I just chose her. The dream came with the package."

And isn't that how love works?
We choose someone, and everything connected to them becomes part of our story; their fears, their hopes, their ambitions, their struggles, their wins, their losses, their becoming.

He didn't fall in love with a restaurant.
He fell in love with a woman who had vision.
And because she had vision, he learned to see farther than he ever planned.

That day at the picnic table, I realized something:

Sometimes the most beautiful love stories don't start with fireworks or magic.
Sometimes they start with a dream; one person holding it, and the other person saying:

"Let me help you carry it."

This chapter wasn't just about falling in love.

It was about falling into purpose together.

And the more he talked, the more I understood that the next
part of his story wasn't about sacrifice…
It was about partnership.

Which leads us into the heart of what he shared next.

Chapter 4

The Yoke Is Even: What Partnership Really Means

Partnership is one of those words people throw around lightly, like it magically appears once two people exchange rings or sign a lease together. But anyone who has lived long enough knows the truth: partnership isn't automatic. It's intentional.

And it sure isn't always equal.

Some couples say they're partners, but one person is pulling life like a mule while the other is riding in the wagon, waving like royalty. Some relationships look balanced from the outside, but behind closed doors the weight is falling entirely on one person's shoulders.

But what my friend described that day at the picnic table? That was something different. Something rare. Something he called an **even yoke.**

Now, before we go any further, let me explain the yoke for anyone who didn't grow up hearing that term in church or in country living. A yoke is a wooden beam used to connect two animals, usually oxen, so they can pull a load together. But here's the secret:

If one animal is stronger than the other, the yoke becomes uneven.

If one walks too fast, the other gets dragged.

If one walks too slow, the other gets strained.

If they aren't moving at the same rhythm, the load becomes heavier.

But when the yoke is even, when both animals walk side by side, matching pace, matching strength, sharing weight; the load becomes manageable. The journey becomes smoother. The destination becomes reachable.

That's partnership.

My friend didn't just marry a woman with a dream. He married a woman who was willing to match him step for step.

"We pulled life together," he said. "Not perfectly. But evenly." He said the early days were rough; not because they didn't love each other, but because they had to learn each other's rhythm. She moved fast. He moved methodically. She wanted to jump in. He wanted to plan first. She cooked from instinct. He measured everything. She worked from passion. He worked from structure.

"And let me tell you," he said, laughing, "you learn real partnership the first time you try to run a business together. That's when all the pretty stuff gets out of the way."

You could tell they had their arguments; the kind you only have with someone who matters. The kind where the disagreement isn't about the issue, but about trying to be understood.

He talked about nights they stayed up arguing about menus, marketing, finances, and who forgot to order flour. He said they both had strong opinions and strong personalities and sometimes they collided like two mountain goats on a cliff.

"But here's what kept us balanced," he said. "We didn't try to be right. We tried to be fair."

Fairness, that was their secret.

They didn't keep score.

They didn't measure sacrifice like it was a competition.

They didn't turn mistakes into weapons.

Every decision they made, they made together, even when it was uncomfortable.

"Being evenly yoked isn't about doing the same things," he said. "It's about carrying the same responsibility for the life you're building."

One day she burned a huge batch of chicken and wanted to shut the whole restaurant down because she was frustrated.

He showed up early the next morning and cooked until his arms were tired.

Another time he made a business miscalculation that cost them money, and she didn't blame him. She rolled up her sleeves, worked twice as hard that week, and said, "We'll make it up. Keep going."

That's the even yoke — not perfection, but shared effort.

He told me about times when one of them was tired or discouraged, and the other had to carry more weight, but only temporarily, never permanently. They didn't allow one person to carry the burden all the time. They rebalanced their life like you rebalance a load in a wagon, gently, intentionally, before something breaks.

"I knew her limits," he said. "And she knew mine."

He laughed when he said this part:

"You can love someone and still drive them crazy. But when the yoke is even, you come back to the middle."

The "middle" that was their sacred ground.

Not her way, not his way, the middle.

Where compromise didn't feel like sacrifice.

Where listening replaced stubbornness.

Where pride didn't lead, but humility did.

Where love didn't just promise, it participated.

He said something I'll never forget:

"Being evenly yoked doesn't mean we always agreed. It means we never let disagreement separate us."

They argued, but they stayed.

They disagreed, but they communicated.

They stumbled, but they rebalanced.

They struggled, but they fought together, not against each other.

That's what made their partnership last.

He talked about how people assume love is the reason couples stay together. But in reality, plenty of couples love each other and still fall apart because they don't know how to carry life together. They love each other, but they don't partner well.

Love alone is the spark. Partnership is the fuel.

Then he said something soft, almost like a confession:

"I didn't become the man she needed by changing who I was.

I became that man by growing into who I could be."

And that right there?

That's emotional maturity.

That's purpose-driven love.

That's the quiet strength that turns a relationship into a legacy.

He looked around the park again, at the kids, the cousins, the elders, the laughter, the food, the conversations floating on the breeze and said:

"This is the proof that we were evenly yoked. Not the restaurant. Not the money. Not the house. **This;** the family, the love, the continuity. That's the result of two people pulling life in the same direction."

I sat there listening, taking in the depth of what he was saying, and I realized something:

Being evenly yoked isn't about matching strengths; it's about matching commitment.

One person can cook.

One person can manage.

One person can lead.

One person can dream.

But if both people pull with equal heart; the life they build becomes unstoppable.

Partnership is not 50/50.

Some days it's 80/20.

Some days it's 30/70.

Some days it's "I don't have anything left," and the other says, "Lean on me."

The yoke stays even not because the weight is equal, but because the dedication is.

Their story wasn't perfect, but it was balanced.

It wasn't flawless, but it was fair.

It wasn't easy, but it was shared.

And the legacy they created; the generations playing around

us, laughing, eating, living, was born from that balance.

Partnership makes love sustainable.

Balance makes love peaceful.

And an even yoke makes love last.

Chapter 5

The Dream He Buried… and Later Resurrected

Every person walking this earth has a dream they tucked away somewhere. Some bury it deep, pretending they forgot. Others fold it up neatly like an old photograph and place it in the back of the closet, hoping one day they'll have the courage to take it out again. But most people; whether they admit it or not, are carrying a dream that life interrupted.

My friend was no different.

Long before the smoke, the seasoning, the busy Saturdays, the endless orders, and the "your ribs changed my life" compliments, he dreamed of something simpler. Something quieter. Something peaceful.

He wanted to travel.
Not just vacation travel. Soul travel.
Meet-people-you-don't-share-a-language-with travel.
Sit-on-a-mountain-with-a-camera-and-breathe travel.

He wanted to take pictures; not selfies, not staged shoots, but the kind of photos that tell the truth about life.

The kind that stop time. The kind that show how big the world really is.

"It wasn't just a hobby," he told me. "It was who I was. Or who I thought I was going to become."

But love stepped into the picture, literally, and flipped the script.

"I didn't stop dreaming," he said. "I just paused it."

People love to romanticize sacrifice, as if giving something up automatically makes you noble. But the truth is, sacrifice only feels holy when it's done with love, not resentment. He didn't bury his dream with bitterness. He tucked it away gently, like placing a delicate keepsake in a drawer.

"I just knew her dream needed more of me at the time," he said. "It wasn't time for mine yet."

That kind of wisdom doesn't come easy.
Most people think sacrifice equals loss.
He understood that timing equals investment.

He didn't destroy his dream; he put it on layaway.

Then he said something that made me stop:
"Some dreams don't die. They just wait for you to grow into the version of yourself that can handle them."

That hit me.

Because how many of us have tried to chase something we weren't mature enough, stable enough, or grounded enough to pursue? How many of us had dreams that would've taken us out if we'd had them too early?

Sometimes God protects you from your own timing.

He told me that in his twenties, he wanted to travel the world with ten dollars and unlimited ambition. But that version of him would've come home broke, disappointed, and with a suitcase full of regret, or worse, never come home at all.

"But the version of me now?" he said, smiling. "I can enjoy it without stress. Without guilt. Without thinking about bills or rushing back."

That's the beauty of a resurrected dream; it comes back upgraded.

He went on to tell me about the day his dream resurfaced.
It wasn't dramatic. No movie scene. No sudden revelation.

It happened quietly, the way most life-changing things happen.

Their kids were grown.
The restaurant had become stable.
Life wasn't a hustle anymore.
The noise had settled.

And one morning, he woke up and thought,
"I think it's time."

His wife agreed without hesitation.
Because love, real love, doesn't forget what your heart once wanted.
Even if you forget, your partner doesn't.

"She said, 'Go. Take your camera. I want you to have that part of your life too.'"

That moment sealed it.

Everything he had given, every long morning, every late night, every sacrifice, every compromise, they came full circle. He wasn't a man trying to escape responsibility. He was a man finally returning to a dream he had earned.

He started small.
A road trip here, a weekend getaway there.
Then bigger trips; the kind that require passports, planning, and a suitcase packed a week early.

And guess what?
He became the photographer he always wanted to be; but with a better eye, a richer life, and a deeper sense of appreciation.

"When I travel now," he told me, "I don't feel like I'm running away. I feel like I'm breathing."

There was something sacred in the way he said that.

He explained that sometimes you need to grow through life before you can appreciate the dream you once had. He didn't want to take pictures because he was chasing freedom. He wanted to take pictures because he finally felt free.

Then he said:

"I'm glad my dream didn't come true back then. It wouldn't have meant the same."

When he travels now, he isn't alone. His wife goes with him. The same woman whose dream he helped build now holds his hand while he fulfills his.

And they no longer travel with tight budgets or cheap hotel rooms or worrying about missing work. They travel with ease, peace, and gratitude because they built the life that makes that possible.

"My dream didn't die," he said. "It matured. And it came back at the perfect time."

That's when I realized something important:

The dream you bury for love doesn't disappear.
It grows roots.
And when it comes back, it comes back stronger.

His life wasn't a story of sacrifice.

It was a story of divine timing.

A story of patience meeting purpose.

A story of love making room for every dream, hers first, his later.

Some people chase dreams.

Some people wait for dreams.

But the wise ones?

They build a life strong enough that their dreams know where to find them again.

And his dream, the one he buried, found him at just the right moment.

Chapter 6

Building a Family, a Legacy, and a Life Worth Keeping

Legacy is one of those words people often associate with fancy bank accounts, big last names, or historical monuments. But if you've ever sat at a family reunion surrounded by four generations laughing, arguing, cooking, teasing, and loving one another in one place, you understand that legacy lives in something much humbler and far more powerful:

Legacy lives in the life you build day by day.

Watching that family reunion unfold was like watching a living tapestry; threads woven from decades of choices, sacrifices, forgiveness, traditions, and stories. You could see the resemblance between people who had never met before. You could feel the rhythm of generations beating in the same heart.

My friend looked at all of it, the kids running around, the elders telling stories, the cousins reconnecting, the food stations smelling like home and said quietly:

"This is our legacy. This is everything we built."
Not the restaurant.
Not the money.
Not the accomplishments.
Not the awards.
Not the titles.

But this, the people.

The life they created. The love they nurtured. The family they raised. The traditions they protected. The moments they didn't even know would matter someday.

He told me that when they first started out, they weren't thinking about legacy. They were just thinking about surviving the day; getting the business running, paying bills, raising kids, balancing life and marriage, and trying not to burn dinner after a 12-hour shift.

Legacy felt like a word for older, wealthier people; not two young adults scraping together a dream with hope and determination.

"But somewhere between struggle and stability," he said, "you start to realize you're building something bigger than yourself."

He watched their kids grow up in the restaurant; doing homework in the back booth, trying to help serve tables, learning responsibility, understanding discipline. He joked that half the kids in their family learned math not from school, but from counting change behind the register.

He talked about how their family meals weren't fancy, but they were consistent and consistency becomes culture. They told the same old stories, laughed at the same old jokes, argued about the same old things, and showed up for each other in ways that built emotional safety.

"That's legacy," he said. "Showing up; even when life is loud, even when life is hard, even when things aren't perfect."

Then he told me about the early years when money was tight and they didn't have much, but they always made room at the table for anyone who needed a meal. Their home became a place where nephews, cousins, neighbors, and friends of friends could eat, talk, find comfort, or just feel seen.

He laughed and said, "Sometimes I didn't know half the people sitting at my table, but she knew all their stories."

That was the beginning of their community; not just kinfolk but chosen family.

Legacy is not built by blood alone.
Legacy is built by love, consistency, and kindness repeated over time.

He said something that stuck with me:

"Your reputation is what people say about you. Your legacy is what people live because of you."

This family reunion; with hundreds of people, was living proof of the life they lived.

As we sat at that picnic table, he pointed out people:

"That's my nephew; he learned how to cook from us."

"That's my cousin's child; her first job was in our restaurant."

"That young girl there? Her grandmother used to work with us."

"That man over there? He moved to this state because of a job I recommended."

"That older lady? We used to bring her meals when she couldn't leave the house."

He wasn't bragging. He was remembering.

Remembering the small choices that grew into lifelong connections.
Remembering the times love asked for more, and they gave it.
Remembering the moments they could've walked away, but stayed.
Remembering that nothing they built happened overnight.

He said that legacy isn't created intentionally, not at first. It grows quietly behind the scenes, forming its foundation in ordinary days.

"The legacy we leave," he said, "comes from how we lived, not what we owned."

Their family wasn't perfect. They had disagreements, generational misunderstandings, old wounds, new lessons, and personalities big enough to fill the entire park. But love held them together, and legacy gave them identity.

Then he smiled and said, "And now? Now we get to enjoy the fruit of all those hard years."

He talked about watching his children become parents and leaders.
Watching his grandchildren grow into themselves.
Watching younger relatives carry traditions without being asked.
Watching his wife's recipes passed down and perfected.
Watching his once small, uncertain dream turn into a family anchor.

And then almost as if he was speaking to himself, he whispered:

"We built a life worth keeping."

A life full of:

Holidays where everyone showed up

Birthdays that turned into entire productions

Family who argued but apologized

Kids who grew up knowing they were loved

A home filled with warmth, noise, and belonging

A marriage that weathered storms and stayed standing

A dream built together, not alone

That is legacy.

Legacy is not just what you leave behind; it's what continues while you're still here. It's the peace you feel when you look around at your life and say, "We did something right."

As we sat there, watching four generations eat, laugh, hug,
tease, dance, and live out the values he and his wife instilled,
I realized something powerful:

Legacy is the visible evidence of invisible work.

The quiet sacrifices.
The hard conversations.
The early mornings and late nights.
The forgiveness that gets no applause.
The commitment that goes unseen.
The love that grows, expands, and multiplies.

Their legacy wasn't in the food.
It wasn't in the pictures.
It wasn't in the successful business.

Their legacy was the family.
And that family was the story they wrote together, day by day,
choice by choice, year by year.

When he looked at that reunion, he didn't just see people.
He saw his life.

And in that peaceful moment, under that maple tree, I understood exactly what he meant when he said:

"This is what love becomes."

Chapter 7

Happiness: Redefined, Rebuilt, and Relearned

Happiness is one of those words everyone uses but few people truly understand. When you're young, happiness looks like excitement; travel, freedom, adventure, ambition, and big dreams that stretch across the whole sky. But the older you get, the more you realize that happiness changes shape. It matures alongside you. It becomes quieter, deeper, steadier.

My friend sat at that picnic table with the peace of a man who understood happiness in its most honest form. Not the kind you chase. The kind you grow into.

He told me that when he was younger, happiness meant movement; going somewhere, doing something new, seeing something he'd never seen before. He wanted the world. He wanted adventure. He wanted experiences that made his heart race. There's nothing wrong with that. Most of us start there.

But life has a way of teaching you that real happiness isn't always loud.
Sometimes it's the softest thing in the room.

He laughed as he explained it:

"Back then, happiness was adrenaline. Now? Happiness is peace. And peace feels better than anything I chased in my twenties."

That truth hit me hard.

Because if you live long enough, you eventually reach a point where chaos, drama, noise, uncertainty, and emotional roller coasters no longer feel exciting, they feel exhausting. You stop wanting what looks good and start wanting what feels good. You stop chasing temporary highs and start protecting lasting calm.

He said he relearned happiness over the years, not because he planned to, but because life revealed new definitions.

Happiness Definition #1: Peace Over Performance

He used to feel pressure to be impressive, to prove himself, to hit certain milestones by a certain age. But one day, he woke up and realized he didn't need an audience for his life to matter.

"Now," he said, "my favorite sound is quiet."

Not empty quiet, peaceful quiet. The kind of quiet where your spirit settles and your thoughts stop running. The quiet you feel when you know you're where you're supposed to be.

Happiness Definition #2: Being Seen Without Pretending

When he met his wife, he felt seen. Not "seen as potential," but seen as a whole person. Loved, flaws included, growth included, becoming included.

"When someone knows your heart better than you do," he said, "that's real happiness."

He didn't have to perform. He didn't have to hide. He didn't have to present a version of himself for acceptance.

Happiness became authenticity, not perfection.

Happiness Definition #3: Building Instead of Chasing

He said something so true, I nearly wrote it down on a napkin:

"Happiness stays longer when you build it instead of chase it."

Chasing happiness gives you moments.
Building happiness gives you a life.

He built his happiness through partnership, children, shared goals, late-night talks, early-morning responsibilities, laughter, prayer, forgiveness, and slow growth.

Not glamorous. Not Instagram-worthy.
But beautiful — deeply beautiful.

Happiness Definition #4: Loving the Life You Built
There was a time he wondered if he gave up too much. But as he got older, he realized he hadn't given anything up, he had paved the road for the life he lives today.

They travel now, the way he once dreamed of.
He takes pictures now with a better eye and a fuller heart.
He rests now, without worrying about bills or deadlines.
He enjoys now, without guilt or pressure.

"This version of happiness," he told me, "is richer because it's rooted in gratitude."

He learned that happiness becomes deeper when it grows from seeds you planted years ago. The love, the sacrifices, the effort, they all bloom in their own time.

Happiness Definition #5: The Freedom to Slow Down
He said, "I don't need adventure every day. Some days I'm happy just waking up with peace."

The man who once wanted the world now finds joy in:

Cooking breakfast at home

Listening to his wife hum while she gets ready

Family gatherings

Quiet evenings

Sitting on the porch

Traveling without stress

Taking photos of simple things, a flower, a sunset, a street market, a quiet river.

His happiness isn't about proving anything.

His happiness is about being present.

Happiness Definition #6: Watching Your Legacy Live

He pointed at his grandchildren playing and said,

"Happiness is seeing your love walk around in the next generation."

I felt that.

Because when you live long enough, happiness becomes more about what continues after you than what happens to you.

Watching his children become adults, watching grandchildren grow, watching traditions continue, watching love multiply — that brought him joy he couldn't have imagined in his youth.

Happiness Definition #7: Realizing You Chose Right

He smiled while watching his wife laugh with family, her joy still contagious after all these years.

"There's a special kind of happiness," he said, "in realizing you chose the right partner.

We weren't perfect, but we grew right."

I nodded, because that kind of truth sits heavy. The kind of heavy that feels like gratitude.

When you choose someone who grows with you, not away from you; happiness becomes easier. Staying becomes easier. Life feels lighter. Love feels safer.

Happiness Definition #8: Loving Yourself Through Every Season

He said something quietly, almost in reflection:

"I'm happy with who I've become."

And that, right there, is the final evolution of happiness.

Not happiness because of things.
Not happiness because of other people.
Not happiness because life finally got easier.

But happiness because you've made peace with the choices you made and the person you grew into.

He didn't become the photographer he imagined in his twenties.

He became something better, a man with depth, purpose, maturity, stability, and peace.

He didn't get the life he dreamed of.
He got the life he built.
And it was better.

Before we packed up to leave that picnic, he looked around at everything, the food, the laughter, the generations — and said:

"I used to chase happiness. Now, happiness sits beside me."

And that's when I knew:

Happiness isn't found.
Happiness is formed.
And the most beautiful kind is shared.

Chapter 8

Everlasting Love: The Life You Build Together

There is a moment in every long-lasting relationship when you look around at the life you've built and realize something profound: love didn't stay because it was easy; it stayed because the two of you chose each other, over and over, through every season.

As the day at the family reunion drew to a close, my friend and I sat in a comfortable silence, the kind only years and wisdom can create. The sun was slowly lowering itself behind the trees, casting a warm glow across the park. Kids were still playing tag, elders were gathering their belongings, music drifted into the breeze like a soft farewell, and the smell of charcoal and fried fish lingered in the air like a memory.

He looked over at his wife across the field; laughing, joking, making sure everyone had food to take home, hugging the people who tried to sneak out early. She had the same energy she probably had the day he fell in love with her: alive, confident, connected, present. The kind of woman whose joy fills any space she enters.

With tenderness in his voice, he said,
"That's my girl... the same one I chose decades ago. And choosing her is still the best decision I've ever made."

There was no showmanship in his tone. No performance. It was the kind of truth that sits in the bone.

Everlasting love isn't loud.
It isn't dramatic.
It isn't perfect.

It's steady.
It's reliable.
It's patient.
It's grown, not gifted.

He told me that real love isn't measured in butterflies or chemistry, though those things have their place. Real love is measured in what you build, what you protect, what you nurture, and what you return to when life gets heavy.

"It's not that we didn't have storms," he said. "It's that we didn't let the storms drown us."

They had years where they barely recognized themselves.

Years where money was tight.

Years where communication felt like speaking two different languages.

Years where parenting demanded everything.

Years where they struggled to stay aligned.

Years where dreams shifted and life felt uneven.

"But we didn't give up," he said. "We fixed the yoke. We adjusted. We talked. We prayed. We healed. And we learned."

That's everlasting love.

Not a love without challenges but a love strengthened because of them.

He said something that gave me chills in the most unexpected way:

"Every couple changes. The trick is to make sure you don't change into strangers."

That line stayed with me.

Because long-term love requires renewal; the willingness to meet the new version of your partner without longing for an old version that no longer exists. It also requires humility, understanding that you, too, will change, and someone must be willing to choose the new you.

He talked about how they didn't try to keep the relationship the same. They grew it. Let it evolve. Let it breathe. Let it expand. Let it bend without breaking.

He shared how they reinvented themselves multiple times:

As young partners figuring out life

As parents learning responsibility

As business owners learning survival

As grandparents learning joy

As older adults learning rest

Every chapter of their life required a different version of them, and they were willing to meet those versions with grace, not resistance.

"Everlasting love is not one story," he said. "It's a collection of them."

They had seasons of passion, seasons of purpose, seasons of fatigue, seasons of healing, seasons of change, seasons of peace. And together, they made room for each one.

He looked back toward the picnic crowd, his eyes soft, reflecting the quiet satisfaction of a man who lived well and loved deeply.

"That's why I say this... this family, this peace, this life; it's what love becomes when two people honor each other."

His words made something very clear:

Everlasting love isn't built in the big moments, the weddings, the anniversaries, the milestones.

It's built quietly, consistently, in the everyday choices:

Cooking dinner after a long day

Laughing at inside jokes from fifteen years ago

Holding hands during hard times

Apologizing first

Listening with intention

Not weaponizing mistakes

Choosing kindness

Protecting each other's peace

Dreaming together

Forgiving without keeping score

It is the sum of a thousand small moments done with a full heart.

He leaned in and said the words that summed up his whole life:

"Love becomes legacy when it lasts long enough to teach the next generation what love looks like."

And when I looked at those four generations; the babies, the teens, the adults, the elders, I realized he was right. They weren't just celebrating family. They were celebrating the result of shared commitment.

Love had duplicated itself through the generations.
Love had traveled through time.
Love had built something bigger than both of them.

And that, right there, is the beauty of everlasting love:

When you get it right, it outlives you.

As the evening wrapped up and we stood to leave the picnic table, he looked around once more, his eyes filled with gratitude, and said:

"This is what love becomes... when you treat it right."

A legacy.
A family.
A story worth telling.
A life worth keeping.

And with that, he walked toward his wife; the love he chose, the dream he supported, the partner who carried the yoke beside him, and I realized that the story wasn't just about him.

It was about every person who chooses love with intention, patience, and purpose.

Because when you do...

This is what love becomes.

As this journey comes to a close, I hope you see what I saw that peaceful summer afternoon under the maple tree: that love is not just a feeling; it is a lifelong construction project. A sacred building. A legacy shaped piece by piece, year by year, choice by choice.

Love starts as hope.
It grows into commitment.
It becomes partnership.
And eventually, if tended carefully, it becomes legacy.

The story shared in these chapters wasn't perfect. It wasn't glamorous. It wasn't free of struggle or sacrifice. It was something deeper: real.

Real love that adjusts.
Real love that forgives.
Real love that grows.
Real love that rebalances the yoke when life tilts too far to one side.
Real love that lets dreams rest and resurrects them at the right time.
Real love that builds family, culture, and continuity.

Real love that evolves into peace.

Because when all the excitement settles, when the kids grow up, when the business stabilizes, when the storms pass, and the noise finally quiets...

You're left with the person beside you.
The life you built.
The memories you created.
The legacy that echoes.

And that; that is what love becomes.

Not the fireworks of the early days, but the calm of the seasoned ones.
Not the picture-perfect moments, but the steady moments.
Not the grand gestures, but the everyday kindness.
Not the pursuit of happiness, but the peace of being understood.
Not the loud declarations, but the quiet choosing, again and again.

Everlasting love isn't about avoiding the hard seasons.
It's about staying connected through them.

This book is a reminder that love is an evolving story.

A collaboration.

A partnership with many chapters.

Some messy.

Some beautiful.

All necessary.

And when done right, love grows beyond the two people who first felt it.

It becomes part of the next generation.

It becomes tradition.

It becomes memory.

It becomes legacy.

So as you close these pages, may you carry this truth with you:

Love becomes bigger than you when you honor it, nurture it, and let it expand through the life you build together.

May your own love; past, present, or future, find its rhythm.

May your dreams align with someone who sees you deeply.

May your sacrifices bloom in the right season.

May your partnerships stay balanced.

And may your legacy be one worth keeping.

Because this —
this is what love becomes.

Why I Wrote This Book

There are moments in life that speak louder than anything we plan. Sitting at a picnic table on a quiet summer afternoon, listening to a man reflect on decades of love, sacrifice, and partnership, I realized I was witnessing something rare, a living example of what love becomes when two people treat it with respect, intention, and care.

This book was born from that moment.

I wrote this book to honor the quiet stories that often go untold, the stories of everyday people who build extraordinary lives through patience, commitment, forgiveness, and shared effort. Not perfect love, but grown-up love. Not fantasy-filled love, but love that lasts, evolves, and strengthens across generations.

I wrote it because so many of us forget that love is more than emotion. It's more than a spark. It's more than chemistry.

Love is a choice.
Love is a daily practice.
Love is the legacy we leave behind.

In telling his story, I wanted to capture the beauty of partnership, the courage of compromise, the resurrection of forgotten dreams, and the power of building a life with someone who walks beside you, not ahead, not behind, but beside.

My hope is that these pages remind you that real love is possible.
Real partnership is possible.
Real legacy is possible.

And that when we honor love with maturity and intention... it becomes something far more beautiful than we ever imagined.

Helpful Resources

Whether you're seeking deeper understanding of love, relationships, partnership, or personal growth, these resources can support you on your journey:

Books & Guides by Vgdawson

When Love Lets Go

Silent Tears of a Mother's Heart

Boundaries with Family and Friends

Dear Self: Reflections and Resilience Across Life's Journey

The Dating Smart Collection (for teens and parents)

I Need to Think About My Life Choices

Parenting Through Generations

The Holiday Blues Collection

And many more at www.what2buynext.com

Supportive Tools for Personal Growth

Journals & guided reflections

Dating Smart workbooks

Vision board templates

Aromatherapy candle collections designed to support healing, self-care, and emotional balance

Community & Emotional Wellness

Consider joining local relationship workshops

Seek support from couples counselors or relationship coaches

Explore online communities focused on healing, partnership, and building healthy relationships

Remember: seeking growth, clarity, and support is a sign of strength; never weakness.

Stay Connected with Me

This isn't goodbye. This is just the beginning.

If this book spoke to your soul, I invite you to join my inner circle, a place for women (and men) who are ready to grow, heal, and walk in truth together.

Subscribe to the "Letters from vgdawson" Newsletter
Get exclusive reflections, behind-the-scenes writing updates, journal prompts, book releases, and self-care tools delivered straight to your inbox.

 Sign up at: www.what2buynext.com/newsletter
Follow on Social Media:
Instagram | YouTube | TikTok: @what2buynext
Website: www.what2buynext.com

Together, let's keep writing new chapters.
Chapters of peace, purpose, and power.
You deserve every bit of it.
Warmly,

Vgdawson

The Truth About Aging

What Your 50s, 60s, and 70s Will Show

Vgdawson

The Truth About Aging offers a clear, faith-grounded examination of what time reveals — in your body, your finances, your relationships, your emotional patterns, and your walk with God.

This is not a fear-based book about getting older.

It is a steady Christian perspective on how decades of habits, decisions, and beliefs compound — and how God remains faithful through every season.

Aging is not sudden.

It is accumulated.

In your 50s, the shift begins.

In your 60s, the audit becomes clearer.

In your 70s, refinement is unavoidable.

But aging is not only physical or financial — it is spiritual.

Author of books on relationships, personal growth, and life transitions.

Friendship is one of the most
powerful relationships we
experience in life—
yet it's often the one we
understand the least.
**In *Friends for Life: How to
Grow and Keep Friendships
for a Lifetime*, you're invited**
into an honest, soul-centered
conversation about what it
truly means to build

friendships that last. This is not a book about surface-level
connections or temporary companionship. It's about the friends who
walk with you through seasons of growth, change, joy, and
heartbreak—and the wisdom it takes to nurture those bonds with
intention.
Whether you're cherishing lifelong friends, navigating shifting
connections, or learning how to be a better friend yourself, *Friends for
Life* meets you where you are. It reminds you that meaningful
friendship doesn't happen by accident—it's built through presence,
honesty, and care.
This book is for anyone who believes that friendship is not just a part
of life, but one of its greatest gifts.

Author of books on relationships, personal growth, and life transitions.

Thank you for taking this journey with me.

Thank you for opening your heart to this story — a story of love shaped over decades, of dreams shared, of sacrifices honored, and of a legacy built through patience, partnership, and devotion.

Writing this book was a heartfelt experience, and knowing you spent your time reading these pages is an honor I do not take lightly.

Thank you for supporting my work, my voice, and my mission to write stories that uplift, encourage, and remind us that love — real love — is still alive in this world.

May your own journey be filled with peace, purpose, and the kind of love that grows deeper with time.

With gratitude,

Vgdawson